EAT LO

© 2017 ACC Editions
World copyright reserved

ISBN: 9781851498734

Published in French under the title:
*Eat Londres: 85 adresses incontournables pour voyageurs gourmands*
© Tana éditions, a department of Edi8, Paris, France – 2016
ISBN: 9791030101225

The right of Annabelle Schachmes to be identified as author of this work has been
asserted by her in accordance with the Copyright, Designs and Patents Act 1988

British Library Cataloguing-in-Publication Data

A catalogue record for this book is available from the British Library

The author and publisher gratefully acknowledge the permission granted to reproduce
the copyright material in this book. Every effort has been made to trace copyright
holders and to obtain their permission for the use of copyright material. The publisher
apologises for any errors or omissions in the text and would be grateful if notified of any
corrections that should be incorporated in future reprints or editions of this book.

Graphic design: Lisa Magano

Printed in Spain for ACC Editions, an imprint of ACC Art Books Ltd,
Woodbridge, Suffolk, England
www.accartbooks.com

# EAT LONDON

## THE 85 TASTIEST ADDRESSES

ANNABELLE SCHACHMES

ACC EDITIONS

When you first arrive in London, nothing can beat the warm, cosy atmosphere of a British pub. Order yourself a beer, tuck into a pie, a Scotch egg or a plate of sausage and mash, and take in the spectacle around you. Over the last few years, this city has been undergoing a transformation. It has become a real melting pot of flavours. In just a few decades, London has managed to combine a well-established European gastronomic culture with the madness of Anglo-Saxon cuisine, drawing upon the culinary traditions of the many different nationalities that call this place home. Take for example the restaurant Hook, which redefines the traditional fish and chips by giving it new textures and tastes inspired by world cuisine, or the numerous street food markets such as Broadway or Maltby Street, which offer an enormous variety of dishes. Factor in the city's virtuoso young chefs, such as those at The Clover Club, Story or especially the Mirror Room at the Rosewood Hotel, and there is no denying that London has entered a whole new culinary sphere.

So if I can offer you one piece of advice, it is to taste whatever takes your fancy. After all, eating is a way of exploring the world!

# CONTENTS

# SHOPS
# AND
# FOODSTORES

# CHOCCYWOCCYDOODAH

30-32 FOUBERTS PL, W1F 7PS
☎ (0)20 7734 9713 ⊖ Oxford Circus

MONDAY–SATURDAY: 10 am–7 pm • SUNDAY: 10 am–6 pm
🍫 to 🍫🍫🍫 depending on the product

HTTPS://WWW.CHOCCYWOCCYDOODAH.COM   🅵 🆈 🅾

This shop is almost like a museum of chocolate sculpture, so monumental are its chocolate creations. It is full of exceptional cakes, realised in exquisite detail. You can also buy chocolate bars and individual chocolates (sea salt, cinnamon), lollipops or figures made out of different chocolates. The enormous popcorn lollipops dipped in white or milk chocolate will make your mouth water! On the first floor, there is a café decked out in Alice in Wonderland style décor, where you can sample the specialities of the house.

# BOOKS FOR COOKS

4 BLENHEIM CRESCENT, NOTTING HILL, W11 1NN
☎ (0)20 7221 1992 ⊖ Ladbroke Grove then 70 bus to Portobello Road bus stop

**TUESDAY–SATURDAY**: 10 am–6 pm

HTTP://WWW.BOOKSFORCOOKS.COM

If you like cookery books, this is a nice little shop for a browse. You will find a fine selection of English cookbooks on an impressively wide range of topics, from breakfast to classic British cuisine, with recipes for cannabis mug cakes thrown in for good measure! At the back of the shop, you can get a cup of tea and a salad or a slice of cake in the charming café. If you go on a Saturday, you can drop in on Portobello Road market, which is on the doorstep.

---

# MY CUP OF TEA

5 DENMAN PL, W1D 7AH
☎ (0)20 7287 2255 ⊖ Piccadilly Circus

**MONDAY–FRIDAY:** 10 am–7 pm • **SATURDAY:** 11 am–7 pm • **SUNDAY:** 12–5 pm
Closed every day 1–1.30 pm

HTTPS://WWW.MYCUPOFTEA.CO.UK

Nestling in one of the back streets behind Piccadilly Circus you will find a veritable Aladdin's Cave of tea. With teas from many different countries in Asia (China, Japan, India and Sri Lanka), you are bound to find one to suit your palate. There are teas for every meal of the day (breakfast, afternoon tea, etc.), but also teas for special occasions, such as Jade Oolong from Taiwan, with its subtle flavours and slight hint of bitterness. Then there are the classic teas and blends such as Earl Grey, Darjeeling or Genmaicha, and smoked or perfumed teas (Earl Grey with its hint of lavender, blackcurrant tea...) There is also a fine selection of herbal teas for sale.

# FORTNUM & MASON

181 PICCADILLY, W1A 1ER
☎ (0)20 7734 8040 ⊖ Piccadilly Circus or Green Park

**MONDAY–SATURDAY:** 10 am–9 pm • **SUNDAY:** 11.30 am–6 pm

HTTPS://WWW.FORTNUMANDMASON.COM          ▮ ▮ ▮

Famous for the quality of its products, Fortnum & Mason is a real symbol of British culture. This food, tableware and home store has been the official supplier of numerous royal courts over the last 150 years. They are the grocer by appointment to Her Majesty Queen Elizabeth II, and supply tea to the Prince of Wales. It's a must-visit destination for foodies coming to London. Legend has it that Fortnum & Mason invented a number of British specialities, such as the Scotch egg. And in 1886 the store was the first to import what would become a staple of the English breakfast: baked beans (or haricot beans in tomato sauce).

# PAXTON & WHITFIELD

93 JERMYN ST, SW1Y 6JE
☎ (0)20 7930 0259 ⊖ Piccadilly Circus or Green Park

MONDAY–SATURDAY: 10 am–6.30 pm · SUNDAY: 11 am–5 pm

Consult the website for other locations

HTTP://WWW.PAXTONANDWHITFIELD.CO.UK                    [f] [◎]

For more than 200 years, Paxton & Whitfield, cheesemonger by appointment to the Queen, has been sourcing and maturing exceptional cheeses. In their shop in Piccadilly Circus, not far from Fortnum & Mason, you will find a large selection of British and international cheeses. They also stock a full selection of products to complement their cheese. At the back of the shop there is an impressive shelf of cheese dishes and utensils.

# GILL WING COOK SHOP

190 UPPER ST, N1 1RQ
☎ (0)20 7226 5392  ⊖ Highbury & Islington

**MONDAY–SATURDAY:** 9.30 am–6 pm  •  **SUNDAY:** 10 am–6 pm

Consult the website for other locations

`HTTP://WWW.GILLWING.CO.UK/KITCHEN/`                    ﬀ ﹀ ⊙

If you love cooking utensils, your heart will leap for joy when you walk through the doors of this shop. You will find every possible utensil you could need for cooking, and a few you've never even thought of. Pots and pans (in cast iron and stainless steel) of every shape and size, knives, brushes for scrubbing vegetables... There are more than 2,000 separate items to choose from!
A little further up the street there is another Gill Wing, which is more of a gift shop. On display is a collection of teapots that belonged to the former proprietor. It's not for sale, but is still well worth making a detour for, since most of the pieces are no longer available and are as original as they are sublime!

# HARRODS

87-135 BROMPTON RD, SW1X 7XL
☎ (0)20 7730 1234 ⊖ Knightsbridge

**MONDAY–SATURDAY:** 10 am–9 pm  •  **SUNDAY:** 11.30 am–6 pm

`HTTP://WWW.HARRODS.COM`      📘 🐦 📷

Harrods is a real London institution, and it's as essential a part of your itinerary as Buckingham Palace. Its food hall, which consists of a number of rooms each as beautiful as the last, is an impressive sight. It's no surprise that Harrods places so much emphasis on food, as its founder, Charles Henry Harrod, first set up as a grocer and specialist tea wholesaler in the suburbs of London more than 150 years ago. Each room is decorated with superb mosaics or frescos painted on the walls and ceilings. You can buy any number of souvenirs with the name of the shop on the label, but equally you can get fresh produce (fruit, vegetables, meat, fish), pre-prepared meals or pastries and confectionery. You can also tuck into a platter of oysters, a grilled steak or an Asian dish in one of the nine restaurants inside the store.

# LA FROMAGERIE

2-6 MOXON ST, W1U 4EW
☎ (0)20 7935 0341 ⊖ Baker Street or Regent Park

MONDAY–FRIDAY: 8 am–7.30 pm  •  SATURDAY: 9 am–7 pm
SUNDAY: 10 am–6 pm

Consult the website for other locations

HTTP://WWW.LAFROMAGERIE.CO.UK

Patricia Michelson, the owner of this establishment, developed her love of cheese in Méribel, France. She brought back a whole wheel of Beaufort to England and sold it by the slice from market stalls. In September 1992 she opened her first branch of La Fromagerie in Highbury Park, followed by a second in November 2002 in Mayfair. This second branch is much bigger than the first. It has an impressive cheese cellar, and in it you will find a large selection of cheeses from many different countries – England, naturally, but also France, Germany, Switzerland and Spain. The shop also sells vegetables and other products to complement their cheese. Next door at number 6 is the La Fromagerie restaurant, where you can sample cheeseboards of French, Italian or Swiss cheeses washed down by carefully selected wines, but also salads and roast meats. Tart and fondue evenings regularly take place on Thursdays.

# SELFRIDGES FOODHALL

400 OXFORD ST, W1A 1AB
☎ 0800 123400 ⊖ Bond Street

**MONDAY–SATURDAY:** 9.30 am–9 pm • **SUNDAY:** 11.30 am–6 pm

HTTP://WWW.SELFRIDGES.COM/GB/EN/CAT/FOODHALL/                    ⨍ 🐦 📷

A few hundred metres from Oxford Circus, the food hall of the famous department store Selfridges is a very good way to sample the wares of several emblematic London companies. For example, you will find chocolates from the famous chocolatier Charbonnel et Walker, takeaway dishes and salads from Baker & Spice and cupcakes from Lola's. You can also tuck into ramen at Tonkotsu, take traditional afternoon tea at Dolly's, enjoy a platter of oysters and a glass of champagne at the Prunier counter or have breakfast at Forest (the restaurant on the roof), or in any one of the other twelve restaurants on site.

# ROCOCO CHOCOLATES

5 MOTCOMB ST, SW1X 8JU
☎ (0)20 7245 0993  ⊖ Knightsbridge

**MONDAY–SATURDAY:** 8.30 am–7 pm  •  **SUNDAY:** 11 am–6 pm

---

3 MOXON ST, W1U 4EW
☎ (0)20 7935 7780  ⊖ Baker Street or Regent Park

**MONDAY–SATURDAY:** 10 am–6.30 pm  •  **SUNDAY:** 10 am–5 pm

Consult the website for other locations

**HTTPS://WWW.ROCOCOCHOCOLATES.COM**

  ꘐ 𝕏 ⬚

You will find a large selection of sweets and chocolate bars in these lovely old-school sweetshops, arranged across brightly coloured displays. In partnership with the Grenada Chocolate Company, Rococo grows its own cocoa beans. These are made into unique organic chocolate bars, which contain the characteristic notes of Caribbean cocoa. There is also a collection of dark, milk and white chocolates, as well as bars with more original flavours such as cinnamon, Moroccan mint, white cardamom, rose, orange and stem ginger, and even basil and Persian lime. Not to mention the wide range of sweets for special occasions (Easter, Christmas, Mother's day, etc.) or just for everyday enjoyment.

# NEAL'S YARD DAIRY

COVENT GARDEN SHOP, 17 SHORTS GARDENS, WC2H 9AT
☎ (0)20 7240 5700 ⊖ Covent Garden

**MONDAY–SATURDAY:** 10 am–7 pm

---

BOROUGH MARKET SHOP, 6 PARK ST, SE1 9AB
☎ (0)20 7367 0799 ⊖ London Bridge

**MONDAY–FRIDAY:** 9 am–6 pm • **SATURDAY:** 8 am–6 pm

Consult the website for other locations

HTTPS://WWW.NEALSYARDDAIRY.CO.UK

The speciality of this cheese shop is that they only sell cheeses from the British Isles: they distribute the products of around forty cheesemakers from the United Kingdom and Ireland and mature them in the shop. The only exception to this is brie from Meaux. While the cheeses are maturing in their cellar they are constantly tested and tasted to monitor their development. You will discover different sorts of Cheddar (Montgomery Cheddar is just out of this world), soft cheeses, goat's cheese and blue cheese (you simply have to try the Stichelton – you'll never taste anything like it). Their yogurts and cream cheeses are quite exceptional.

# WHOLE FOODS MARKET

63-97 KENSINGTON HIGH ST, THE BARKERS BUILDING, W8 5SE
☎ (0)207 368 4500  ⊖ High Street Kensington

**MONDAY–SATURDAY:** 8 am–10 pm  •  **SUNDAY:** midday–6 pm (the restaurant closes 30 minutes before the shop closes)

🛍 to 🛍🛍🛍 depending on the product

Consult the website for other locations

`HTTP://WWW.WHOLEFOODSMARKET.COM/STORES/KENSINGTON`    f ⊙

Whole Foods Market is a chain of supermarkets known around the world for its natural and organic products and its commitment to sustainable agriculture. The store in Kensington is one of the largest. Spread over three floors, it offers both fresh food and general groceries. For example, you can make your own peanut butter or buy fruit juice that has been freshly squeezed on site. You can choose a bottle of organic wine or beer from their fine selection. Upstairs there is an impressive food court. You can sample, among others, Mexican or vegetarian specialities. Kensington Whole Foods Market is a great shop for browsing, with lots of things to discover.

# THE SPICE SHOP

1 BLENHEIM CRESCENT, W11 2EE

☎ (0)20 7221 4448 ⊖ Ladbroke Grove, then bus 7 or 70 from bus stop B Ladbroke Grove Station to PA Portobello Road

**MONDAY–SATURDAY:** 10 am–6.30 pm • **SUNDAY:** 11 am–4 pm

HTTP://WWW.THESPICESHOP.CO.UK                                    f

Just opposite Books for Cooks, on a little street in Notting Hill, is this small shop with its range of over 2,500 spices. Its range includes individual peppers, but also traditional spice mixes from distant lands (such as the Baharat spice mixture, which is very well known in the Middle East but difficult to find in Europe). The shop also offers spicy sauces, curry paste and cocktail ingredients. If you can't locate it anywhere else, you'll find it here.

# TURNER & GEORGE

399 ST JOHN ST, CLERKENWELL, EC1V 4LB
☎ (0)20 7837 1781 ⊖ Angel

MONDAY: 10 am–4 pm • TUESDAY–FRIDAY: 10 am–7 pm
SATURDAY: 10 am–5 pm

HTTPS://WWW.TURNERANDGEORGE.CO.UK    f 🐦 ⓘ

A brand specialising in quality British meat. They have nine varieties of beef (Longhorn, Angus, Hereford, etc.), five of lamb and mutton (Herdwick, Texel, etc.) and six of pork (Oldspot, Tamworth, etc.) from animals reared under strict conditions by local producers, to optimise the maturing of the meats in the shop (which takes at least ten days). Whatever the type of meat, the result is a taste sensation.

You can also buy incredible sausages and sliced bacon in vacuum packs (very handy if you want to take some home).

# MARKETS

# BOROUGH MARKET

8 SOUTHWARK ST, SE1 1TL
☎ (0)20 7407 1002  🚇 London Bridge

**MONDAY–THURSDAY:** 10 am–5 pm  •  **FRIDAY:** 10 am–6 pm
**SATURDAY:** 8 am–5 pm
Some stalls are closed on Mondays and Tuesdays

`HTTP://BOROUGHMARKET.ORG.UK`                                    🄵 🄾

Borough Market is without doubt the biggest tourist magnet of all London's food markets. The reason: you can fulfil all your culinary needs. Here you can shop for fruit and vegetables, meat, fish or cheese, eat a real English breakfast while leaning on a counter (the fresh crumpets and muffins are out of this world), share a beer with friends or sample a zebra-meat burger, a Scotch egg or some spit-roasted pulled pork.

On Saturdays try to get here early (before 10.30) or arrive towards the end of the market, since at peak times the market is heaving.

Don't forget to explore the back streets around the market. You'll find some real gems, such as Sausage World, a restaurant that specialises in freshly pan-fried, succulent sausages.

# BRICK LANE MARKET

91 BRICK LN, E1 6QR

⊖ Aldgate East then bus 67 from bus stop F Aldgate East to S Shoreditch High
Street Station

**SATURDAY:** 11 am–6 pm • **SUNDAY:** 10 am–5 pm

`HTTP://WWW.BRICKLANEMARKET.COM`    **f** **y**

A giant flea market takes place at the weekend, covering the entire length of
Brick Lane. At the top of the street (near the Cereal Killer Café and Beigel Bake)
the stalls are geared towards clothes and knick-knacks. The bottom end,
however, offers an impressive range of street food stalls of every description.
You will find a barista in a totally reconfigured London taxi whose roast coffee
will enchant you. You can sample Canadian poutines or toasted cheese sandwiches. A bit further down the street is the Old Truman Brewery, where the
street food market continues, with stalls selling specialities of Ethiopia, Japan,
etc. For those with a sweet tooth, we strongly recommend the refreshing
chocolate fruit kebabs from the Choco Fruit stall.

# BROADWAY MARKET

FROM LONDON FIELDS PARK TO REGENT'S CANAL, E8 4QJ

⊖ Bethnal Green then bus 106 or254 from bus stop C Bethnal Green Station to R Mare Street/Victoria Park Road

**SATURDAY:** 9 am–5 pm

HTTP://BROADWAYMARKET.CO.UK

This kaleidoscope of tastes and cultures is our favourite market, and is without doubt one of the most picturesque in London. It takes place every Saturday morning in the street of the same name in the borough of Hackney. You can buy fruit and vegetables and cheese, but also a huge number of specialities that you can enjoy on the spot. For example, you simply have to taste the toasted Cheddar and haggis sandwiches, or lobster rolls made with freshly caught fish from the English coast. The market runs the whole length of the street and there are also numerous food shops, restaurants, pubs and cafés to draw you in. As you walk look out for the signs pointing to Schoolyard Market (more or less in the middle). This little side market takes place in the playground of a neighbouring school and is completely dedicated to street food.

# MARYLEBONE FARMERS' MARKET

CRAMER STREET CAR PARK, MARYLEBONE, W1U 4EW

Baker Street or Regent's Park

**SUNDAY:** 10 am–2 pm

Consult the website for other locations

HTTP://WWW.LFM.ORG.UK/MARKETS/MARYLEBONE/

A farmers' market really is the best way to understand local produce, because a number of small artisans and producers are gathered together in a single place. This is not just classic greengrocer's produce: on the 40-odd stalls at the farmers' market at Marylebone you will find an apple grower who makes incredible juices (Chegworth Valley Juices), sublime cakes at the Honeypie Bakery stall (you absolutely have to taste the courgette, lime and pistachio) and outstanding cheeses from the Bath Soft Cheese Company. Make sure to check out http://www.lfm.org.uk, as there are other farmers' markets that take place at weekends all over London.

# GLOBAL KITCHEN AT CAMDEN MARKET

54-56 CAMDEN LOCK PLACE, NW1 8AF

⊖ Camden Town

**MONDAY–SUNDAY:** 10 am–6 pm

HTTP://WWW.CAMDENLOCKMARKET.COM/FOOD-DRINK/GLOBAL-KITCHEN/

**f** 🐦 ⊙

A bit like Borough Market, Camden Market is quite the tourist trap. You are strongly advised to go there on a weekday if you can, because it's difficult to move through the crowds at a weekend. But that's not to say that this market doesn't have an interesting selection of street food. Just a few paces past the sign saying 'Welcome to Camden Lock' you will find a small square studded with street food stalls. This is the Global Kitchen. You can sample Polish sausages, mountain specialities from Tibet and Jamaican jerk chicken. Make sure you continue onwards through the market. You will come across other street food stalls, as well as brands such as Honest Burgers and Chin Chin Labs (ice creams made before your eyes with the aid of liquid nitrogen). The stall not to be missed is Cookies and Scream. Their cookies, brownies and cupcakes are simply delicious.

# MALTBY STREET MARKET

LASSCO ROPEWALK, 41 MALTBY ST, SE1 3PA

☎ (0)20 739 48061  🚇 Bermondsey then bus 47, 188 or 381 from bus stop A
Bermondsey Station to E Dockhead

**SATURDAY:** 9 am–4 pm  •  **SUNDAY:** 11 am–4 pm

🍲 to 🍲🍲 depending on product

HTTP://WWW.MALTBY.ST                                    f 🐦 ◎

Every weekend a cute little street food market takes place in the commercial arcades of Lassco with typically English specialities such as Scotch eggs and pies from the Finest Faire stall, and home-made Scottish smoked salmon at the Hansen & Lydersen stall. As well as these, there are loads of other stalls selling foreign food, such as The Toucan with its Brazilian cuisine and the sensational sausages from Herman Ze German. You can buy products directly from their producers, such as sauces from the Whisky Sauce Company, but also fruit, vegetables and home-made juices. Under the arches opposite the stalls there are some lovely shops and restaurants such as Monty's Deli, famous for its pastrami, and Market Gourmet, well known for its seafood and accompanying wines. Make a note of the stalls that feed you the best, as many of them have their own Facebook and Instagram pages.

# SPA TERMINUS

DOCKLEY ROAD INDUSTRIAL ESTATE, DOCKLEY RD, SE16 3SF
Ⓣ Bermondsey

**SATURDAY:** 9 am–2 pm
🍴 to 🍴🍴🍴 depending on product

HTTP://WWW.SPA-TERMINUS.CO.UK                    ⨍ 🐦

Spa Terminus is just a few hundred metres from Maltby Street Market. As a continuation of the latter, under the arches, there are thirty or so shops/showrooms belonging to producers of wines, meats, beers, cheeses, vegetables, coffee, honey and other products for special occasions. They are open during the week and cater exclusively to restaurant professionals. However, on Saturday mornings, they open to the public rather than the initiated. The latter give out the address rather sparingly, as the place is something of a secret.

# POP BRIXTON

49 BRIXTON STATION RD, SW9 8PQ
☎ (0)20 3879 8410 🚇 Brixton

**SUNDAY–WEDNESDAY:** 9 am–11 pm  •  **THURSDAY–SATURDAY:** 9 am–midnight

HTTP://WWW.POPBRIXTON.ORG

Pop Brixton is a community space, a hothouse of talent and independent artists. Made from repurposed multi-coloured containers, the place includes multiple design and fashion enterprises. But most important of all are the twenty street food stalls: incredible pizzas by Made of Dough, spiced popcorn/kebabs by Viet Box, smoked beef sandwiches by The Bell & Brisket and amazing tacos by Maria Sabina. Pop Brixton is a place of culinary discovery where you can enjoy a moment among friends. A community farm has recently opened there too, where it is possible to grow all sorts of fruit, vegetables and aromatic herbs. This part is open to local residents and restaurateurs who wish to grow their own produce.

# MERCATO METROPOLITANO

42 NEWINGTON CAUSEWAY, SE1 6DR
☎ (0)20 7403 0930  ⊖ Borough

**TUESDAY–SATURDAY:** 11 am–11 pm • **SUNDAY:** 10 am–9 pm
🍱 to 🍱🍱 depending on the product

HTTP://WWW.MERCATOMETROPOLITANO.CO.UK                    f 🐦 ⓞ

At the Underground station near Borough Market you will come across a most unexpected sight. Just inside the entrance you will fall under the spell of a large top-quality Italian food shop with a selection of general food, meat and cheese sold loose as in a delicatessen. But the real show-stopper is next door, in the huge space where dozens of street food stalls have set up. Raclettes, pizzas (with the most divine dough), burgers (using dry aged meat), Vietnamese, Spanish and British specialities and even a wine merchant make for a festival of flavours. Not to be missed under any circumstances is the van belonging to Bellini & Oyster, with divine oysters from small British producers which you can sample accompanied by different versions of Bellini made from their wines. Another part of Mercato Metropolitano not to be missed is the Backyard Cinema. Reserve your seat in advance via their website (www.backyardcinema.co.uk) and you will be in for an exceptional experience; you can watch your favourite film, with a drink in your hand or eating an ice cream, reclining on a beanbag in a unique setting.

# TEATIME

# CUTTER & SQUIDGE

20 BREWER ST, W1F 0SJ

☎ (0)20 7734 2540 ⊖ Piccadilly Circus

**MONDAY-WEDNESDAY:** 9.30 am–8 pm · **THURSDAY:** 9.30 am–9 pm
**FRIDAY:** 9.30 am–10 pm · **SATURDAY:** 11 am–9 pm · **SUNDAY:** 11 am–8 pm

🍱 🍱

HTTP://CUTTERANDSQUIDGE.COM

Biskies – little sandwiches made from shortbread biscuits – are the speciality of the house. With their attractive decorations and flavoured cream fillings, they are served at teatime in pretty three-tiered bamboo bowls. My choice would be the crème brûlée flavoured biskie, cheesecake, and Earl Grey tea – each cuter than the last, and all very tasty. There are also savoury sandwiches with exotic flavours and smoked cheese scones, as well as other sweet treats: cream cake, house marshmallows, brownies, ice cream... For hot drinks, you can choose from a selection of home-made or herbal teas. The venue is light and pleasant and just a stone's throw from Piccadilly Circus.

# DOMINIQUE ANSEL

17-21 ELIZABETH ST, BELGRAVIA, SW1W 9RP
☎ (0)20 7324 7705  ⊖ Victoria

**MONDAY–SATURDAY:** 8 am–8 pm • **SUNDAY:** 9 am–8 pm
🎂 to 🎂🎂 depending on the dessert

HTTP://DOMINIQUEANSELLONDON.COM

🅵 🆈 🅾

It would be easy to disregard this cake shop and say: 'Oh yeah, it's everywhere! Seen it a thousand times.' But think again, hombre! You'd be missing a great eating experience. Every Dominique Ansel shop is unique. Aside from classics such as the Cronut® (which you'll need to order in advance online) or the S'More (you have to try it!), there are a number of original creations on offer. When in London, go there for a classic tea, which you can liven up with one of the exclusive pastries of the establishment such as a quite outstanding revised version of the famous Eton Mess (the flavours and textures are incredible) or a Paris–London (a novel version of the famous Paris–Brest) composed of an Earl Grey flavoured mousse, lemon curd and a chocolate ganache. For those with a taste for the savoury, make sure you try the Welsh Rarebit Croissant, the Kedgeree Croquettes (with a base of smoked haddock and semi-boiled quail's egg) or the traditional Chicken Belly Pot Pie.

**Eton Mess Lunchbox**
(London Exclusive)
Mousse & jam 'strawberries', mini meringues, basil, black pepper & Fromage Blanc. Shake me up and make a mess!
£7.50

GF

**Paris – London**
(London Exclusive)
Our twist on the Paris–Brest, with Earl Grey mousse, lemon curd and blackberry ganache
£6.20

# PEGGY PORSCHEN CAKE

116 EBURY ST, SW1W 9QQ
☎ (0)20 7730 1316 🚇 Victoria

**MONDAY–SUNDAY:** 10 am–6 pm
🎁🎁

HTTP://WWW.PEGGYPORSCHEN.COM

Decorated entirely in pink, Peggy Porschen's has the look of a sweet shop. The shop specialises in wedding cakes, but inside you can sit and enjoy a selection of sandwich cakes filled with cream or jam, with an incredible sponge as soft as down. You can also sample delicious cupcakes, divine little jammy dodgers, artisan teas or a glass of champagne. The perfect place for tea with charm!

# BISCUITEERS

194 KENSINGTON PARK RD, W11 2ES

☎ (0)20 7727 8096 ⊖ Ladbroke Grove then bus 7 or 70 from bus stop B Ladbroke Grove Station to PA Portobello Road

MONDAY–SATURDAY: 10 am–6 pm  •  SUNDAY: 11 am–5 pm

🍱 to 🍱🍱🍱 depending on product

HTTP://WWW.BISCUITEERS.COM/BISCUITEERS-SHOP-ICING-CAFE-NOTTING-HILL

🅕 🅞

Little savoury sandwiches and traditional cakes (scones, macaroons, mini-cupcakes), but also colourful and creative specialities of their very own – these are the teatime treats in store at this pretty black-and-white shop in Notting Hill, a temple of cookie icing. That is to say, not only can you buy cookies decorated with the face of your favourite celebrity or to celebrate a particular occasion (birth, marriage, etc.), you can also learn how to make them yourself thanks to their themed classes, which run throughout the year. Their shop provides all the utensils you need to decorate your own cookies at home.

# SKETCH

9 CONDUIT ST, W1S 2XG
☎ (0)20 7659 4500  ⊖ Oxford Circus

**MONDAY–FRIDAY:** 8 am–2 pm • **SATURDAY:** 10 am–2 pm
**SUNDAY:** 10 am–midnight
🍱🍱🍱

HTTPS://SKETCH.LONDON/  ⬛ f 🐦 📷

Whether served to you in the Gallery (a superb room designed by India Mahdavi, decked out in pink with the feel of a chic brasserie, featuring velvet chairs and banquettes and Art Deco chandeliers) or in the Glade (a smaller room that will transport you to a faraway fairytale world), afternoon tea at Sketch is a fantastic experience. Tea here is a mash-up of traditional elements, such as egg mayonnaise finger sandwiches and scones and jam, and more eccentric ones, such as Malabar® marshmallows, kalamansi (a Japanese citrus fruit) meringues, and raspberry and violet choux pastries. Sketch also provides a special children's menu. To wash down your finger sandwiches or cakes you can choose between tea and champagne. If you select champagne, don't miss out on the Sketch R Tea special. You choose between a Veuve Clicquot or a Pommery selected by Fred Brugues, Sketch's head sommelier. You then get a choice between Earl Grey or vanilla tea. Then, before your eyes, the champagne is poured onto the tea leaves. This lends subtle aromas to the beverage.

# BAKERS
# AND
# CAKE SHOPS

# COCOMAYA

12 CONNAUGHT ST, W2 2AF
☎ (0)20 7706 4214 ⊖ Marble Arch

**EVERY DAY:** 8 am–6 pm

HTTP://WWW.COCOMAYA.CO.UK/    **f 𝕏 ⊙**

Cocomaya is a haven of peace a short distance from Hyde Park. You will feel instantly at home, thanks to the warm and attractive décor. You can come and nurse a cuppa while you do some work, or bring your friends for a proper tea. You'll find it hard to choose between the tasty pastries, cakes and finger sandwiches on offer. Their patisserie is the epitome of comfort food: reassuring, with flavours from your youth, and likely to give you happy flashbacks of childhood teatimes. Cocomaya is a magical place that will take you to another dimension.

# CROSSTOWN DOUGHNUTS

4 BROADWICK ST, W1F 0DA
☎ (0)20 7734 8873  ⊖ Tottenham Court Road

**MONDAY–THURSDAY:** 8 am–10 pm  •  **FRIDAY:** 8 am–11 pm
**SATURDAY:** 9 am–11 pm  •  **SUNDAY:** 9 am–8 pm

Consult the website for other locations

HTTPS://WWW.CROSSTOWNDOUGHNUTS.COM                    

There is a new generation of doughnuts to be had at Crosstown Doughnuts. Light and not too sweet, you can sample doughnuts with classic vanilla toppings or filled with dark chocolate ganache, or raspberry jam. But you could also be tempted by some more original flavours. Depending on the type of doughnut, you might find something akin to the classic fritter recipe (as in the doughnut with strawberry jam and crunchy granola, or the dark chocolate one with little pieces of crystallised chilli on top), or something with a more cake-like texture. This is the case, for example, with the matcha tea doughnut (glazed and filled with a white chocolate matcha ganache). One that you absolutely must try is the weird and wonderful Orange Blossom (date jam, orange and cardamom crumble topping). A positive thing to note: most of these doughnuts are suitable for vegetarians. Make sure you check out their website, as they have stalls at several markets around London.

# FABRIQUE BAKERY

8 EARLHAM ST, WC2H 9RY
☎ (0)20 7240 1392 ⊖ Leicester Sq. or Covent Garden

**MONDAY–FRIDAY:** 8 am–8 pm  ·  **SATURDAY–SUNDAY:** 9.30 am–6.30 pm

---

212 PORTOBELLO ROAD, W11 1LA
⊖ Ladbroke Grove then bus 7 or 70 from bus stop B Ladbroke Grove Station to PA Portobello Road

**EVERY DAY:** 8 am–7 pm

Consult the website for other locations

`HTTP://FABRIQUE.CO.UK`  🇫 📷

The story of Fabrique Bakery began in Sweden, Stockholm to be precise. Once they had opened a dozen or so shops in their native land, they chose Shoreditch as the location for their first London branch. There is nothing industrial-scale about Fabrique. They take the time it takes, use natural fermentation techniques and traditional shaping in order to achieve a flavoursome bread. Their premises are simply decorated, using stripped-back materials. You will find a whole selection of pastries on offer.

# PAVILION BAKERY

18 BROADWAY MARKET, E8 4QJ

☎ (0)20 7241 1241  ⊖ Bethnal Green then bus 106 or 254 from bus stop C Bethnal Green Station to R-Mare Street/Victoria Park Road

**MONDAY–FRIDAY:** 7 am–3 pm  •  **SATURDAY:** 7.30 am–5 pm  •  **SUNDAY:** 8 am–5 pm

This tiny bakery may not look much on the outside, but in the view of many bread lovers it is the best bakery in London. Its display features a selection of superb loaves with golden crusts that will make you want to lick the window pane! Inside, you have a choice of classic leavened loaves and baguettes made with rye flour, but also some superb brioches and a fine selection of pastries, which you can take away with an espresso made on the premises by the Square Mile Coffee Roasters.

# GAIL'S BAKERY

SOHO 128 WARDOUR ST, W1F 8ZL
☎ (0)20 7287 1324 ⊖ Tottenham Court Road

**MONDAY–FRIDAY:** 7.30 am–7 pm • **SATURDAY–SUNDAY:** 9 am–8 pm

Consult the website for other locations

`HTTP://GAILSBREAD.CO.UK`

In these neighbourhood bakeries, bread is the main attraction, and at Gail's Bakery they simply love the stuff. They like to find the very best ingredients to make it, and they like the traditions surrounding it, as much in the eating of it as in the baking of it. And it shows, because the results are simply dazzling! You will find an extensive selection of breads in these shops (classic bread or rye bread, with olives, caramelised garlic, cherry and blackcurrant or indeed rosemary) each as tasty as the next. You can eat on the premises. In the mornings, there is a choice of pastries as well as several specialities, such as the divine shakshuka or bacon and maple syrup brioches, on the breakfast menu. At lunchtime, there are quiches, salads and sandwiches. You must also try their caramelised leek, feta and olive brioches (a sort of brioche version of a pizza). For tea there is a wide choice of savoury finger sandwiches and a large selection of pastries and mini cakes baked on the premises. A top tip: don't leave without sampling their cornbread. Perfectly seasoned, it is served slightly warmed up and crusty. It's a real delicacy! The same goes for their scrumptious and addictive cinnamon buns. Everything is so tasty and moreish, you'll want to eat the whole shop!

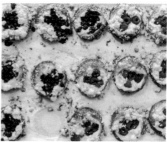

# UDDERLICIOUS

187 UPPER ST, N1 1RQ

☎ (0)20 7359 7777  🚇 Highbury & Islington

**SUNDAY–THURSDAY:** 11 am–11 pm • **FRIDAY–SATURDAY:** 11 am–midnight

HTTP://WWW.UDDERLICIOUS.CO.UK

This little ice cream shop in the heart of Islington has nothing but home-made ices and sorbets made with organic milk from British farms and fresh ingredients. The shop is well known for its bewildering array of flavours, which vary according to the season, such as their famous chocolate and Marmite. Other flavours include mojito, lychee and lemongrass, or peach and prosecco sorbets, and their avocado and choc-chip, or nut, ricotta and honey ice creams. Udderlicious also does delicious ice cream cakes for every occasion.

# MAITRE CHOUX

15 HARRINGTON RD, KENSINGTON, SW7 3ES
☎ (0)20 3583 4561 ⊖ South Kensington

**MONDAY–FRIDAY:** 8 am–8 pm • **SATURDAY–SUNDAY:** 10 am–8 pm
🐷🐷🐷

Consult the website for other locations

`HTTP://MAITRECHOUX.COM`

A truly virtuoso pâtisserie. Joakim Prat worked as pâtisserie chef for a number of large London restaurants, including L'Atelier de Joël Robuchon and the Greenhouse, before launching himself on the adventure that is Maitre Choux. In this shop, he has pulled off a masterstroke by improving French pâtisserie classics, such as the éclair and the choux pastry. He infuses his pastries with a certain French *je ne sais quoi*, which makes them truly exceptional.
Well-chosen ingredients and a matchless technique always make for a winning recipe. Faced with a violet and wild berries éclair or the classic vanilla choux pastry, you will have great difficulty making a choice!

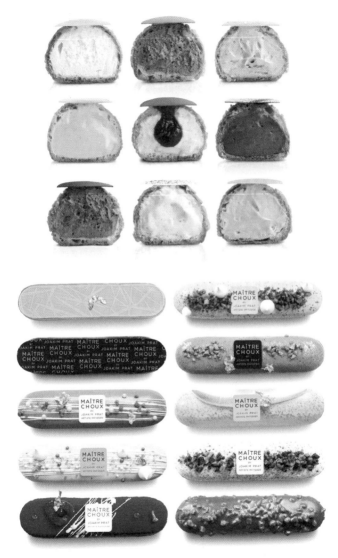

4-40 CARAMEL, SALTED CARAMEL, BUBBLE GUM, VANILLA, CUSTARD
PEANUT BUTTER, LEMON PIE, CHOCOLATE COOKIES

# OR CHOOSE A...
# Cereal
# Cocktail

*, OREOS, ROLOS
PO, CANDY CORN
S, MARSHMALLOWS
ES, MAGIC STARS
ITE CHOC BUTTONS
OWS, CHOC CHIPS
BERRYS, BLUEBERRIES,
CRANBERRIES
S, WALNUTS

LABLE

ST
arts
nks

> EASTER EGGSTRAVAGANZA –

HONEYCOMB, COCOA PEBBLES
MINI EGG, KINDEREGG

> THE LION KING – 4·00

LION CEREAL, COCO CARAMEL SHREDDIES,
ROLOS, CARAMEL MILK.

> PHCPITMS – 4·00

KRAVE, COCO POPS, HAPPY HIPPO,
CHOCOLATE MILK

> DOUBLE RAINBOW – 4·70

FROOT LOOPS, FREEZE DRIED MARSHMALLOWS,
TRIX, STRAWBERRY MILK.

> UNICORN POOP – 4·80

RICICLES, PARTY RINGS, MARSHMALLOWS,
100'S N 100'S, FLUFF, WHOLE MILK

> STICKEY MONKEY – 4·80

TOFFEE CRISP, DIGESTIVE, BANANA, CREAM,
TOFFEE SAUCE, BANNA MILK.

> MN CO CISE – 4·70

WEETOS, CHOCOPIC, AERO MINT BUBBLES,
MINT MILK.

> DIDTEL YOU WAS V8N – 4·70

REECES PUFFS, OREOS,
SOYA MILK.

# BREAKFAST

# E PELLICCI

332 BETHNAL GREEN RD, E2 0AG
☎ (0)20 7739 4873 ⊖ Bethnal Green

**TUESDAY–SATURDAY:** 7 am–4 pm
🍲 to 🍲🍲🍲 depending on the product

HTTP://EPELLICCI.COM

E Pellicci is an address to slip under the table, the ultimate tip-off. The interior is in need of sprucing up, but who cares when you can get a real English breakfast, made up of sausages, bacon, tomatoes, grilled mushrooms and eggs, which you can either have à la carte or put together in a meal, all at the unbeatable price of £5.50. There are some Italian dishes on the lunchtime menu, but dishes are primarily based on British meat.

---

# FOXCROFT & GINGER

69-79 MILE END RD, E1 4TT
⊖ Mile End/Stepney Green

**MONDAY–FRIDAY:** 8 am–10 pm • **SATURDAY–SUNDAY:** 9 am–10 pm
🍲 to 🍲🍲 depending on the product

HTTP://FOXCROFTANDGINGER.CO.UK

A very tasty breakfast is to be had in this welcoming establishment, with its modern/industrial chic décor. Even though there are a few classics like Eggs Benedict, you should not expect to find the traditional English breakfast here. You are more likely to find French toast with ham, mature Cheddar and honey mustard or spiced aubergine tarts with halloumi, labneh, mushrooms, poached egg and peppers. You can eat here at any time of the day, not just at breakfast.

# THE COLONY GRILL ROOM

THE BEAUMON HOTEL – 8 BALDERTON ST, BROWN HART GARDENS,
MAYFAIR, W1K 6TN

☎ (0)20 7499 9499  ⊖ Bond Street

**BREAKFAST EVERY DAY:** 7 am–11.30 am • **BRUNCH WEEKENDS:** 11.30 am–5 pm
**RESTAURANT OPEN EVERY DAY:** 7 am–midnight, except Sundays closes 11 pm
💷💷 to 💷💷💷 depending on the product

HTTPS://WWW.COLONYGRILLROOM.COM                    f 🐦 ⊙

Reminiscent of 1950s America, with a very elegant Art Deco style, this is
the perfect place for a posh breakfast if you have something to celebrate
or an important business meeting. The menu includes a large selection of
pastries, granolas, mueslis, fresh fruit and pancakes. You can have your eggs
done whichever way you like – fried, scrambled, boiled, Benedict, omelette
– alongside salmon, cheese or ham. The star item on the menu is of course
the traditional English breakfast! At the weekend, as well as these breakfasts,
the brunch menu offers a choice of dishes such as steak tartare with chips or
meatloaf with Madeira sauce and truffles.

# CEREAL KILLER CAFE

139 BRICK LN, E1 6SB

☎ (0)20 3601 9100  ⊖  Aldgate East then bus 67 from bus stop F Aldgate East to L Shoreditch High Street/Bethnal Green Road

**MONDAY–SUNDAY:** 8 am–8 pm

---

LEVEL 2, STABLES MARKET, CAMDEN, NW1 8AH

☎ (0)20 3393 8857  ⊖  Camden Town

**MONDAY–SUNDAY:** 9.30 am–7 pm

---

HTTP://WWW.CEREALKILLERCAFE.CO.UK    f 𝕐 ⊙

This place takes you back! Here you will find every breakfast cereal known to man. You can choose between more than 120 different cereals, and thirty varieties of milk ranging from full fat to soya via scented milks (vanilla, mint, peanut butter). You can top up your bowl with chopped nuts, Mini Chamallows® or M&Ms®. One piece of advice: try the cereal cocktails. They are incredible! 'Often imitated but never equalled!' – the atmosphere of Cereal Killer Café is quite unique. If you love the 1980s and 1990s, you really have to go there. The décor, composed of trinkets from this era, is simply mind-boggling.

# ST. JOHN BREAD AND WINE

94-96 COMMERCIAL ST, E1 6LZ

☎ (0)20 7251 0848  ⊖  Aldgate East then bus 67 to Brushfield Street

**MONDAY:** 8 am–9 pm  •  **TUESDAY–SUNDAY:** 8 am–11 pm  •  **SATURDAY:** 10 am–5 pm

🧳 🧳

Consult the website for other locations

HTTPS://WWW.STJOHNGROUP.UK.COM/SPITALFIELDS/                    f 𝕐

Just a short hop from Spitalfields Arts Market, St John Bread and Wine is a unique place with a unique history. Originally it was just the premises where they made bread for their mother restaurant, St John and sold a few bottles of wine. As their customer base has grown, it is now possible have lunch or dinner there, but their pièce de resistance is their breakfast! Whether you have a sweet or savoury tooth, you're spoilt for choice. Toast, porridge, bacon sandwich, ham and eggs, fruit juice – it will be the breakfast of your dreams.

---

# THE BREAKFAST CLUB

31 CAMDEN PASSAGE, N1 8EA

☎ (0)20 7226 5454  ⊖  Angel

**MONDAY–WEDNESDAY:** 8 am–10 pm  •  **THURSDAY–SATURDAY:** 8 am–11 pm
**SUNDAY:** 8 am–10 pm

🧳 🧳

Consult the website for other locations

HTTP://WWW.THEBREAKFASTCLUBCAFES.COM                    f ⌾

If you are really hungry, this is the place for you. From the time that it opens until midday (weekdays) and 5pm (weekends) you can sample the most extravagant breakfasts and brunches in London! Waffles topped with fried chicken drip with maple syrup, and pancakes are sold in piles of four. Not to be missed is their version of the traditional English breakfast, the 'Full Monty': bacon, sausage, black pudding, eggs, chips, mushrooms, baked beans, grilled tomatoes and toast.

# THE SHEPHERDESS CAFÉ

221 CITY RD, EC1V 1JN

☎ (0)20 7253 2463  ⊖ Angel then bus 43, 205 or 214 from bus stop H Angel Islington/City Road to T Moorfields Eye Hospital

**MONDAY–FRIDAY:** 6.30 am–4 pm • **SATURDAY:** 7.30 am–3 pm
🍴 to 🍴🍴 depending on product

🇫 ⊡

If you're after a real English breakfast, this is the place all native Londoners will recommend! In this charmingly old-fashioned café you can order ready-made dishes composed of sausages, bacon, tomatoes, baked beans or black pudding and eggs from a selection of twelve different breakfasts, all at unbeatable prices. There is also a choice of toast and omelettes.

# PUBS
# AND
# DRINKS

# BREWDOG SOHO PUB

21 POLAND ST, W1F 8QG
☎ (0)20 7287 8029 ⊖ Oxford Circus

**MONDAY–THURSDAY:** midday–11.30 pm • **FRIDAY–SATURDAY :** midday–midnight
**SUNDAY :** midday–11 pm
🍺🍺 to 🍺🍺🍺 depending on the product

Consult the website for other locations

HTTPS://WWW.BREWDOG.COM/BARS/UK/SOHO

Right in the heart of London in touristy Soho, not far from Piccadilly, Oxford Circus and Leicester Square, you'll be able to enjoy a beer in the stripped-back ambience of the famous Brewdog bar. The bar is split over two levels and is fitted out with twenty taps serving artisan beers. You're sure to find something here to suit your taste, given the large selection ranging from mild and light beers to the citrusy tang of Dead Pony Club via Punk IPA or the more robust Kingpin. Alongside your beer, we'd strongly recommend the wacky chorizo dog: a brioche roll containing an artisan chorizo sausage, a reduced chilli and almond sauce, smoked garlic mayonnaise, parmesan and small piquillo peppers.

# DIRTY BONES

20 KENSINGTON CHURCH ST, W8 4EP
☎ (0)20 7920 6434  ⊖ High Street Kensington

**MONDAY–THURSDAY:** 5 pm–midnight  •  **FRIDAY–SATURDAY:** midday–1 am
**SUNDAY:** midday–10 pm  •  Brunch at the weekend
🍖🍖 to 🍖🍖🍖 depending on the product

TOP FLOOR, KINGLY COURT, CARNABY ST, SOHO, W1B 5PW
☎ (0)20 7920 6434  ⊖ Piccadilly Circus or Oxford Circus

**MONDAY–THURSDAY:** midday–midnight  •  **FRIDAY:** midday–12.30 am
**SATURDAY:** 11 am–12.30 am  •  **SUNDAY:** midday–10 pm  •  Brunch at the weekend
🍖🍖 to 🍖🍖🍖 depending on the product

HTTP://DIRTY-BONES.COM

Dirty Bones is the temple of comfort food and refined cocktails. It has an unbeatable down-to-earth and relaxed vibe! The main branch in Kensington has bands and DJs performing every night. In the Soho restaurant, the musical ambience is more hip-hop/R&B. It has an impressively original cocktail menu, including Key Lime Pie Martini (a cocktail version of a lemon tart, on which the lime foam is set alight in front of you) and Dirty Mary (a twist on the Bloody Mary, which has a base of tomato juice, lemon, gherkins, pickles, vodka and chilli sauce, with the rim of the glass plunged into crème fraiche and Pringles® crumbs). There is also a selection of comfort food dishes: spare ribs covered in a thick miso and pomegranate sauce, home-made burgers, mac-and-cheese croquettes, hot dogs, either classic or with Asian or Italian flavourings.

# BLACK ROCK

9 CHRISTOPHER ST, EC2A 2BS
☎ (0)20 7247 4580 ⊖ Liverpool Street Station

**MONDAY–WEDNESDAY:** 5 pm–11 pm • **THURSDAY:** 5 pm–1 am
**FRIDAY–SATURDAY:** 5 pm–2 am
🍶🍶 to 🍶🍶🍶🍶 depending on the product

`HTTP://BLACKROCK.BAR`                                    🅵 🆈 🅾

Black Rock is a ground-breaking bar that deconstructs some of the stereo-
types and mystique attached to the world of whisky. This bar, with its plain,
minimalist, contemporary design, takes everything back to basics with its
simple menu of whisky-based cocktails. You don't go to the bar for your drink;
instead, the barmen serve customers sat around a huge trunk, cut from a
185-year-old oak. Inside this trunk two channels have been dug out, in which
two cocktails are aged; these are served directly from small taps fitted into
the trunk itself. Alternatively, you can order one of the cocktails on the menu.
All are whisky based and have been designed to bring out the different taste
profiles of the various regions where the spirit is produced. You can also order
your whisky neat, and compare the whiskies of Scotland, Ireland, America
and Japan, as well as those from independent producers, all available in this
impressive library of whisky, which contains 250 different items.

# THE LYRIC

37 GREAT WINDMILL ST, W1D 7LU
☎ (0)20 7434 0604 ⊖ Piccadilly Circus

**MONDAY–THURSDAY:** 11 am–11.30 pm • **FRIDAY–SATURDAY:** 11 am–midnight
**SUNDAY:** midday–10.30 pm
💷💷 to 💷💷💷 depending on the product or wine

HTTP://WWW.LYRICSOHO.CO.UK

A short hop from Piccadilly Circus in the lively quarter of Soho, The Lyric is an authentic British local. It offers a fine selection of beers, either bottled or on tap, wines and spirits. The atmosphere is totally relaxed, just like being at home. They have genuine pub grub, such as traditional fish and chips, sausage and mash with gravy, braised steaks, and various sorts of beef or chicken pie. It's the perfect place to soak up some typically London atmosphere.

# THE SPREAD EAGLE

141 ALBERT ST, NW1 7NB
☎ (0)20 7267 1410 ⊖ Camden Town

**MONDAY–THURSDAY:** 11 am–11 pm • **FRIDAY:** 11 am–midnight
**SATURDAY:** midday–midnight • **SUNDAY:** midday–10.30 pm
🍷🍷 to 🍷🍷🍷 depending on the product or wine

HTTP://WWW.SPREADEAGLECAMDEN.CO.UK

The Spread Eagle is a pub in the great British tradition. The décor is unique, and the food consists of UK classics (such as a braised lamb pie with red cabbage and pickles, or grilled sausage in onion gravy, or the divine fish and chips), but also nods to international cuisine (as with the Camden Burger). The Spread Eagle is an absolute delight. At lunchtime there is a menu of sandwiches and finger food, and on Sunday, as well as brunch, the famous British Sunday lunch has pride of place, with a choice of meats served with roasted vegetables, goose-fat chips and Yorkshire pudding.

# THE SUN TAVERN

66 LONG ACRE, WC2E 9JD
☎ (0)20 7836 4520 ⊖ Covent Garden

**MONDAY–THURSDAY:** midday–11.30 pm • **FRIDAY–SATURDAY:** midday–midnight
**SUNDAY :** midday–10 pm
🍷🍷

HTTP://WWW.THESUNTAVERNCOVENTGARDEN.CO.UK

Right at the heart of Covent Garden, The Sun Tavern is the ideal place for a leisurely drink with friends while watching a match or having a snack. They serve classic British pub grub, including steak and onion pie, Cumberland sausage with mash, and the traditional fish and chips. This pub is well situated for a number of West End theatres and offers a 'pre-theatre' menu.

# THE GINSTITUTE

PORTOBELLO STAR - 171 PORTOBELLO RD, W11 2DY
☎ (0)20 3588 7800  🚇 Ladbroke Grove then bus 23, 52 or 452 from bus stop B
Ladbroke Grove Station to Elgin Crescent

**TUESDAY–THURSDAY:** 7 pm  •  **FRIDAY:** 2 pm, 5 pm, 7 pm  •  **SATURDAY:** midday,
2 pm, 5 pm, 7 pm  •  **SUNDAY:** 2 pm  •  Gin-making (lasts around 3 hours)
🍸🍸🍸🍸

HTTPS://WWW.THEGINSTITUTE.COM                    ❙f ❙y

The Ginstitute offers a unique, incomparable opportunity to get a better understanding of the true spirit of gin. The experience begins with an historical overview, where a Gin Instructor fills you in on the history of the drink. This covers gin's origin as a medicine, the passionate relationship Britain has had with the drink for the last 200 years and its golden age as a cocktail ingredient. Once the history lesson is over, you move on to the tasting room, where your senses will be enticed by a sample, and an explanation of the key ingredients of London Dry Gin. Once you have learned all there is to know, you can go on to create your own, unique gin to exactly suit your taste. The recipe will be kept securely, so you can order a fresh supply whenever you like. Included within the price for the three-hour session are a bottle of your own blend, a bottle of Portobello Road Gin and four drinks during the session itself.

# THREE EIGHT FOUR

384 COLDHARBOUR LN, SW9 8LF
☎ (0)20 3417 7309  ⊖ Brixton

**MONDAY–FRIDAY:** 5 pm–midnight • **SATURDAY:** 11 am–1 pm
**SUNDAY:** 11 am–midnight • Brunch at the weekend
🍱🍱 to 🍱🍱🍱 depending on the product

HTTP://WWW.THREEEIGHTFOUR.COM                    ❙❙ 🐦 ⭕

Three Eight Four is a bar/restaurant in Brixton where you can drink cocktails
and snack on small savoury or sweet dishes. It's the perfect place to unwind
after a day spent exploring the city! The cocktail list is on a par with those
in large hotel bars, with a few original house specials such as Ziggy Stardust
(Stolichnaya Citros vodka, cassis syrup, egg whites, pomegranate and lemon
juice) and Shiso Mojito (Santa Teresa rum, ginger ale, chilli, cucumber, leaves
of green shiso, and sugar). As for the snacks, they are a fusion of culinary
influences from around the world, as in their steak chimichurri, crispy avocado
wontons and mozzarella arancini.

# BLIND PIG

58 POLAND ST, W1F 7NR
☎ (0)20 7993 3251 ⊖ Oxford Circus

**MONDAY–SATURDAY:** midday–midnight
🍺🍺 to 🍺🍺🍺 depending on the product

`HTTP://WWW.SOCIALEATINGHOUSE.COM`                    🅕

Above the famous restaurant Social Eating House is the bar Blind Pig. There's no sign, just a massive wooden door with a pig's head above it. Inside, you will find a hushed atmosphere, a slightly vintage feel, some old mirrors, wooden chairs with leather banquettes and a range of wild cocktails! The menu is astonishing, and contains some particularly technical cocktails which are perfectly balanced. You can also graze on a range of tapas.

---

# DANDELYAN

MONDRIAN LONDON HOTEL - 20 UPPER GROUND, SE1 9PD
☎ (0)20 3747 1063 ⊖ Blackfriars

**MONDAY–THURSDAY:** 4 pm–1 am  ·  **FRIDAY–SATURDAY:** midday–1.30 am
**SUNDAY:** midday–midnight
🍺🍺 to 🍺🍺🍺 depending on the product

`HTTPS://WWW.MORGANSHOTELGROUP.COM/MONDRIAN/`
`MONDRIAN-LONDON/EAT-DRINK/DANDELYAN`                    🅕🐦

More than just a bar, Dandelyan is a journey of discovery. It provides an experience full of new tastes and unexpected combinations, set in an interior designed by Tom Dixon that combines Art Deco and modern elements, with a view of the Thames to die for. The top man, the multi-award-winning Ryan Chetiyawardana, draws his inspiration from the natural world and offers a range of innovative cocktails as well as some subtle interpretations of classic drinks. The menu has a short description of each cocktail, but also uses simple icons and brief adjectives to explain the dominant flavours of each drink and the best moment to savour it.

# TAKEAWAYS

# DF MEXICO

28-29 TOTTENHAM COURT RD, W1T 1BL
☎ (0)20 3829 2389 ⊖ Tottenham Court Road

MONDAY–SATURDAY: 11.30 am–11 pm • SUNDAY: 11.30 am–10 pm

---

15 HANBURY ST, E1 6QR
☎ (0)20 3617 6639 ⊖ Aldgate East then bus 67 to bus stop S Shoreditch High St

MONDAY–SATURDAY: 11.30 am–11 pm • SUNDAY: 11.30 am–10 pm

HTTP://WWW.DFMEXICO.CO.UK

With its décor combining modern and industrial elements, DF Mexico offers Mexican street food with spicy overtones. You have a large choice of dishes such as burritos, tacos and planchas for sharing. You absolutely have to try the Torta Pork Pibil, a sandwich filled with pork slow cooked on a low heat and marinated in a Yucatan sauce (the recipe is a secret) and seasoned with habanero pepper mayonnaise and pumpkin seeds, washed down by Mexican beer or an iced Margarita. This restaurant is perfectly suitable for someone who doesn't eat meat, as every dish is adaptable to a vegetarian option.

# BEIGEL BAKE

159 BRICK LANE, E1 6SB

☎ (0)20 7729 0616 ⊖ Aldgate East then bus 67 at bus stop F Aldgate East to L-Shoreditch High Street/Bethnal Green Road

**OPEN** 24 hours a day, 7 days a week

Beigel Bake is a real London institution. You are as likely to cross paths with young party-goers seeking a late-night snack as mothers on market days trying to feed their peckish kids. You can buy bagels, pletzels (flat bread with onions) and other forms of bread filled with smoked salmon or the finest salt beef (a smoked beef a bit like pastrami) in London. These slices of pink meat will whet your appetite even before you go in the shop, as they are on display in the shop window. Don't forget to try their cheesecake too – it is especially tasty.

# F.COOKE

9 BROADWAY MARKET, E8 4PH
☎ (0)20 7254 6458  ⊖ Bethnal Green then bus 254 to bus stop R Mare Street

**MONDAY–THURSDAY:** 10 am–7 pm • **FRIDAY–SATURDAY:** 10 am–8 pm

If you're looking for a real British culinary experience, this is the place for you! This local restaurant looks the same as it did when it first opened. The place, the menu (and no doubt most of the customers) haven't changed a bit since the first day. The house speciality is eel, whether on its own, jellied, or accompanied by mashed potato. The menu also includes a range of pies, both savoury and sweet. If you have time, take a stroll afterwards along the canal; it's a pleasant walk when the weather is nice. At weekends you'll find yourself in the thick of the lively Broadway Market.

---

# LARDO

197-201 RICHMOND RD, E8 3NJ
☎ (0)20 8985 2683  ⊖ Bethnal Green then bus 254 to bus stop LQ St Thomas's Square

**MONDAY–SATURDAY:** 11 am–10.30 pm • **SUNDAY:** 11 am–10 pm

`HTTP://WWW.LARDO.CO.UK`

The best pizzas in London, served in a totally chilled-out atmosphere. Here, the emphasis is on the food itself, and this is of the highest quality. The burrata they serve as a starter is soft and creamy, the arancini are crusty and soft. Lardo's food is no-frills and gets straight to the point. Their pizzas are quite simply divine. The dough is matured for a long time, and the ingredients used are exceptional. Our favourite pizza: fennel sausage! What makes some of these pizzas so original is that it is not always tomato sauce that is used to coat the dough. Sometimes it is replaced by cream or even pumpkin purée.

# DINERAMA

19 GREAT EASTERN ST, EC2A 3EJ

☎ (0)20 7033 3903  ⊖ Old Street then bus 135 or 205 from bus stop K-Shoreditch Fire Station to B Shoreditch High Street Station

THURSDAY–SATURDAY: 5 pm–late

🍱 to 🍱🍱 depending on the product

Consult the website for other locations

HTTP://WWW.STREETFEASTLONDON.COM/WHERE/DINERAMA     f 𝕐 ⊙

A real personal favourite! Dinerama is fun, but not too over the top, a great place to spend an evening with friends or even meet a date. Arrive early in the evening if you want to have a snack and a few drinks in a laid-back atmosphere. You'll be able to sample the crème de la crème of London street food from a dozen or so stalls selling pizzas, smoked meats, tacos, fritters and other sandwiches. As the evening wears on the atmosphere warms up. The clientèle changes, families giving way to happy thirty-somethings, and the place takes on the feel of a nightclub late at night. On the roof there is a wine bar and a cocktail bar. The place has an urban vibe and is decorated with containers painted in bright colours and large tables made of untreated wood. Some bits of it are outside and others under cover, so you can have fun here whatever the weather.

Make sure you check out their website, because the owners, the Street Feast company, run three other similar sites across London.

# HOOK

63-65 PARKWAY, CAMDEN, NW1 7PP
☎ (0)20 3808 5112 ⊖ Camden Town

**MONDAY–THURSDAY:** midday–3 pm / 5 pm–10 pm
**FRIDAY–SATURDAY:** midday–10.30 pm • **SUNDAY:** midday–10 pm

HTTP://WWW.HOOKRESTAURANTS.COM  ■ ▼ ⊙

Childhood friends Simon Whiteside and Barry Wallace have created a 'remastered' fish and chip shop. Don't come here expecting anything traditional! Your fish and chips come in little wooden boxes and are served with a choice of breadcrumbs, either fine (crusty panko, similar to the breadcrumb of a Milanese escalope), simple and flavoured with spices, or a smoother tempura, with lemon and basil or chilli and lime. You can choose from several different types of fish (coalfish, haddock, etc.). The sauces (Berber ketchup with sweet potato, spiced mango and lime, chimichurri and more) will take you round the world, and their chips are just spot-on. Apart from the traditional minty mushy peas, the side dishes are equally unconventional (pickled seaweed and shoots, calamari and apple salad, curry and mustard seed). The décor is all wood, a little reminiscent of a fisherman's cottage with a modern twist.

# THE MAYFAIR CHIPPY

14 N AUDLEY ST, W1K 6WE
☎ (0)20 7741 2233  🚇 Bond Street

**MONDAY–SATURDAY:** 11 am–10.30 pm  •  **SUNDAY:** 11 am–9 pm
🥡 🥡 🥡

HTTP://WWW.MAYFAIRCHIPPY.COM                                    ⓕ ⓨ ⓘ

A finalist in the National Fish and Chips Award 2016, the Mayfair Chippy is among the cream of fish and chip shops. Their batter is thick and crunchy and their fish melt in the mouth, a sign of the top quality of their food. Their chips (more like French fries) are tasty and crisp. The portions are served in little metal baskets on a plank of wood, accompanied by simply divine dishes of tartar sauce, mushy peas and curry sauce. On the menu, there are other fried fish such as haddock, but also prawn tails and seafood: dishes of oysters and little pots of mussels. Indulge yourself with some other British specialities such as savoury pies and, for dessert, sticky toffee pudding. The surroundings are very elegant. On the wall there are watercolours of marine specimens; on the floor there are black and white tiles. The overall effect is of a chic bistro.

# POPPIE'S FISH & CHIPS

6-8 HANBURY ST, E1 6QR
☎ (0)20 7247 0892 ⊖ Aldgate East then bus 67 from bus stop F Aldgate East to
S-Shoreditch High Street Station

---

30 HAWLEY CRESCENT, NW1 8NP
☎ (0)20 7267 0440 ⊖ Camden Town

---

55 OLD COMPTON ST, W1D 6HW
☎ (0)20 7734 4845 ⊖ Leicester Square

---

**MONDAY–THURSDAY:** 11 am–11 pm • **FRIDAY–SATURDAY:** 11 am–11.30 pm
**SUNDAY:** 11 am–10.30 pm
🍴🍴

HTTP://POPPIESFISHANDCHIPS.CO.UK                    f 🐦 📷

Grabbing a bite at Poppie's Fish & Chips is a bit like travelling back in time. Even the décor adds to the effect, since it consists of objects reminiscent of the childhood of the shop's owner, Pat 'Pop' Newland, and of the 1950s in general. This is pure traditional British cooking – fish and chips, of course, as the name of the shop indicates, but that's not all. There are other classic dishes on the menu, such as steak or chicken pie and puddings for dessert. The Cartmel sticky toffee pudding is quite unforgettable!

# NANBAN

426 COLDHARBOUR LN, SW9 8LF
☎ (0)20 7346 0098 ⊖ Brixton

**MONDAY:** 5 pm–11 pm • **TUESDAY–THURSDAY:** midday–3 pm / 5–11 pm
**FRIDAY:** midday–3 pm / 5 pm–1 am • **SATURDAY:** midday–1 am
**SUNDAY:** midday–10 pm
🍱🍱 to 🍱🍱🍱 depending on the product

HTTP://WWW.NANBAN.CO.UK                                      f 𝕏 ⊚

With its spare, Japanese-inspired design, Nanban is a temple of fusion cooking. This restaurant draws its inspiration both from Kyushu, the small island in the Japanese archipelago (where ramen, karaage and curry reign supreme) and the very colourful Brixton market in the nearby side streets. Their Salmon Kake-ae (salmon and pickles) and Lamb Tan Tan Men (roasted lamb ramen marinated in Sichuan pepper in a chilli and sesame stock) are to die for. They are also famous for their knock-out cocktails, such as Green Tea Ni (vodka, sake, matcha tea and Cointreau®). But the one you have to drink at least once in your life is the Bloody Mariko, a Japanese version of the Bloody Mary!

# PIZZA EAST

56 SHOREDITCH HIGH ST, E1 6JJ
☎ (0)20 7729 1888 ⊖ Liverpool Street Station then bus 8 or388 from bus stop F
Liverpool Street Station to J Shoreditch High Street/Bethnal Green Road

**MONDAY–WEDNESDAY:** midday–midnight · **THURSDAY:** midday–1 am
**FRIDAY:** midday–2 am · **SATURDAY:** 10 am–2 am · **SUNDAY:** 10 am–midnight

Consult the website for other locations

HTTP://WWW.PIZZAEAST.COM                                           ▮ ▮ ◉

The décor in all three restaurants seems to be straight out of the most up-to-date design magazines. White tiling, recycled wood, and a modern ambience created out of stripped-back materials. The food is part of the décor (a ham hanging above the bar and a wheel of parmesan on display). The menu consists of dishes that are easy to share. From the vegetable antipasti to the sublime pizzas, all the ingredients are of the highest quality. Make sure you don't miss the veal meatballs in tomato sauce and the black truffle, taleggio, parmesan and mozzarella pizza.

# RESTAURANTS

# BOB BOB RICARD

1 UPPER JAMES ST, W1F 9DF
☎ (0)20 3145 1000 ⊖ Piccadilly Circus

**SUNDAY–WEDNESDAY:** 12.30–3 pm/6 pm–midnight
**THURSDAY:** 12.30–3 pm/6 pm–1 am • **FRIDAY–SATURDAY:** 12.30–3 pm/5.30–1 am
🍾🍾🍾 to 🍾🍾🍾🍾 depending on the product and wine

HTTP://WWW.BOBBOBRICARD.COM                     f 𝕐 ◎

The borderline ostentatious chic, the restrained bling – at Bob Bob Ricard they stop just short of going over the top. The two rooms of the restaurant both have their gilded elements. On the menu, they revisit some classics of British and Russian cuisine, such as beef Wellington and vareniki with stuffed potatoes and mushrooms. Bob Bob Ricard has an impressive wine list and is one of the very few establishments in the world (the only one in the UK) that can claim to sell Château Yquem by the glass. But if it's real snob value you're after, you'll find it at every table in the form of a little button you can press to order champagne!

# CEVICHE

17 FRITH ST, W1D 4RG
☎ (0)20 7292 2040 ⊖ Leicester Square

**MONDAY–SATURDAY:** midday–11.30 pm • **SUNDAY:** midday–10.15 pm
🎲🎲 to 🎲🎲🎲 depending on the product

---

2 BALDWIN ST, EC1V 9NU
☎ (0)20 3327 9463 ⊖ Old Street

**MONDAY–THURSDAY:** midday–10.45 pm • **FRIDAY:** midday–11.30 pm
**SATURDAY:** 11 am–11.30 pm • **SUNDAY:** 11 am–9.30 pm
🎲🎲 to 🎲🎲🎲 depending on the product

---

HTTP://WWW.CEVICHEUK.COM                    ◻ ☑ ◻

The chef, Martin Morales, has succeeded in giving traditional Peruvian cuisine a distinctly London twist. You absolute have to sample the ceviches! They are all equally delicious, but one in particular really caught our attention: the Longostino Amazonico, available only in the Shoreditch restaurant. It consists of king prawns marinated in coconut milk seasoned with 'tiger's milk', chara-pita chilli gel, red onions and plantain crisps.

# CHILTERN FIREHOUSE

1 CHILTERN ST, W1U 7PA
☎ (0)20 7073 7676 ⊖ Baker Street

**MONDAY–FRIDAY:** 7.30 am–10.30 am (breakfast)
**MONDAY–WEDNESDAY:** midday–2.30 pm (lunch)/5.30 pm–10.30 pm (dinner)
**THURSDAY–FRIDAY:** midday–3 pm (lunch) • **THURSDAY–SUNDAY:** 6 pm–10.30 pm (dinner)
**SATURDAY–SUNDAY:** 9 am–10.30 am (breakfast)/11 am–3 pm (brunch)
🍴🍴🍴

HTTP://WWW.CHILTERNFIREHOUSE.COM/RESTAURANT/
LUXURY-LONDON-RESTAURANT                                     f

The famous hotelier André Balazs (also the owner of the Mercer in New York) has managed to create a superb hotel in this former fire station, including a restaurant that, with its tiling and blonde wood, large wooden tables and sofas decorated with plump cushions, brings to mind an elegant holiday home in the Hamptons. Nuno Mendes, the chef, has worked with Wolfgang Puck and Jean-Georges Vongerichten. He offers a modern cuisine with international keynotes, such as pavé of grilled salmon with jalapeño pepper béarnaise sauce, octopus and aubergine with daikon radish and mushrooms, or, for brunch, smoked mackerel with kimchi radishes and white cabbage and fried egg.

# CHOTTO MATTE

11-13 FRITH ST, W1D 4RB
☎ (0)20 7042 7171 ⊖ Leicester Square

**MONDAY–SATURDAY:** midday–1.30 pm • **SUNDAY:** 1 pm–midnight
🍱🍱🍱 to 🍱🍱🍱🍱 depending on the product

HTTP://WWW.CHOTTO-MATTE.COM

Chotto Matte is a temple to what is known as Nikkei cuisine. This cuisine is a fusion of two very different cultures, Japanese and Peruvian, which emerged out of the tide of immigration to South America from the beginning of the nineteenth century. Take, for example, the Nikkei Sashimi, which combines in one dish Japanese sashimi and Peruvian prawns. The seasoning for this dish, consisting of a marinade of yuzu and truffles, is simply out of this world. Dinner at Chotto Matte is a quite uncommon sensory experience, mixing dishes with vivid colours and incredible tastes. Dining out in this restaurant on two floors can be a real spectacle, whether you're at the sushi bar or sat in front of the open kitchen where the barbecue is. The cocktail list is impressive, with creations such as Chotto Bellini (peach syrup, white peach, lime, yuzu sake and prosecco) and Flor de Manzana (mango vodka, honjozo sake, apple, lime, passionfruit and elderberry).

# FRENCHIE

16 HENRIETTA STREET, WC2E 8QH
☎ (0)207 836 4422 ⊖ Covent Garden or Leicester Square

**MONDAY–SUNDAY:** midday–2.15 pm/6 pm–10.30 pm
🍱🍱🍱

HTTP://WWW.FRENCHIECOVENTGARDEN.COM

Gregory Marchand is an exceptional chef. You could pick out his dishes from a hundred others. In this London branch of his famous Parisian restaurant you can sample his thoughtful and highly skilled cooking with trademark dishes and ingredients such as smoked meat and fish, but also some new dishes specially adapted for his English restaurant. Gregory Marchand knows London well, having done part of his training at the Savoy Grill, the Electric House and Jamie Oliver's Fifteen. He regards it as a point of honour to use local ingredients: his cheese list, for example, is exclusively English, using produce from the famous cheese shop Neal's Yard. In designing his restaurant, he wanted, with his wife Marie, to create a place that was relaxed and elegant that customers would return to again and again. They entrusted this task to the famous scenographer Emilie Bonaventure, who chose to revisit certain features used in the Parisian restaurant with whitewashed exposed brickwork enhanced by touches of brass, copper and zinc.

# DAYLESFORD

208-212 WESTBOURNE GROVE, NOTTING HILL, W11 2RH

☎ (0)20 7313 8050 ⊖ Paddington then bus 23 from bus stop D Paddington Station / Eastbourne Terrace to PN Colville Road

MONDAY: 8 am-7 pm  •  TUESDAY–SATURDAY: 8 am–9.30 pm
SUNDAY: 10 am-4 pm
🍷🍷 to 🍷🍷🍷 depending on the product and wine

Consult the website for other locations

HTTP://DAYLESFORD.COM/LOCATIONS/NOTTING-HILL-W11/   f 𝕐 ⊙

What began as a passion for authentic food and a simple desire to transform a family farm to provide better nutrition for their children has grown in the past thirty years into one of the most solidly established farms in the United Kingdom. Situated in the Cotswolds, Daylesford is an organic farm that prides itself on its sustainable and responsible approach to agriculture. Daylesford has a number of outlets in London, the largest of which is in Notting Hill, where you can buy fresh food, meat, cheese and yogurts that come directly from the farm. It is also possible to eat in, with a seasonal menu using the farm's produce.

# SALON

18 MARKET ROW, BRIXTON, SW9 8LD
☎ (0)20 7501 9152  ⊖ Brixton

**TUESDAY–FRIDAY:** 6.30 pm–10.30 pm
**SATURDAY:** 10.30 am–3.30 pm/6.30 pm–10.30 pm  •  **SUNDAY:** 10.30 am–3.30 pm
🍲🍲 to 🍲🍲🍲 depending on the product

`HTTP://SALONBRIXTON.CO.UK`

Salon, in Brixton, is a restaurant with an inventive menu based on seasonal products. The dishes are simple, the cooking plain and, above all, locally sourced. Alongside the fixed menu there is an à la carte menu at lunchtime. Especially delicious are the asparagus and poached eggs in smoked butter hollandaise sauce, and the roast lamb with spring greens and anchovies. Their weekend brunch is well worth making a detour for! The dishes are ingenious and appetising, such as smoked salmon scones with beetroot and cabbage slaw, three-cheese cornbread with shredded ham hock, poached eggs and salad, or their stuffed mushrooms with cow's curd and crushed nuts. Salon is a restaurant for having a bite to eat with friends after a morning at the market.

# 108 GARAGE

108 GOLBORNE RD, W10 5PS
☎ (0)20 8969 3769  ⊖ Ladbroke Grove

**TUESDAY–SATURDAY:** midday-3 pm / 6.30 pm–10 pm; closed Sunday and Monday
🍲🍲 to 🍲🍲🍲 depending on the product

`HTTP://WWW.108GARAGE.COM`

This place has all the trappings of a real garage: exposed brickwork and a metal ceiling. The décor is modern; leather chairs accompany tables of wood and steel, and lamps and pictures that look as if they were ferretted out in the nearby Portobello Market. As for the food, thanks to his experience working in some of the world's major restaurants (David Thompson's Nahm in Bangkok, and Enroco Crippa's three-star Piazza Duomo in Alba) the chef, Chris Denney, is able to offer cuisine of extraordinary precision and surprising seasonings, which makes excellent use of seasonal products.

# GRANGER & CO.

STANLEY BUILDING, 7 PANCRAS SQUARE, N1C 4AG
☎ (0)20 3058 2567  ⊖ King's Cross St Pancras

**MONDAY–SATURDAY:** 7 am–11 pm  •  **SUNDAY:** 8 am–10.30 pm
🍱🍱 to 🍱🍱🍱 depending on the product and wine

Consult the website for other locations

HTTPS://GRANGERANDCO.COM                                          f

Bill Granger, the owner, wanted to fashion a restaurant in the image of his native land, Australia – in other words, sunny and generous. This Aussie surfer has come up with some extremely well-balanced menus, with an emphasis on fresh, healthy ingredients. He favours spice-based seasonings over heavy sauces, and interesting combinations of tastes, for example the chia seed pot with almond milk, berries, pomegranate and coconut yogurt (on the breakfast menu), or the chicken, brown rice and coriander and lime broth (served at lunchtime), or the miso, aubergine, crispy tofu and shiso, or the crispy duck, plum, star anise, brown rice and citrus salad.

# HOLBORN
# DINING ROOM

HOTEL ROSEWOOD - 252 HIGH HOLBORN, WC1V 7EN
☎ (0)20 3747 8633  ⊖ Holborn

**MONDAY–FRIDAY:** 7 am–11.30 pm  •  **SATURDAY:** 8 am–11.30 pm
**SUNDAY:** 7 am–10.30 pm
🍱🍱🍱 to 🍱🍱🍱🍱 depending on the product

HTTP://WWW.HOLBORNDININGROOM.COM                              ⓕ ⓞ

With its classic British pub décor, this place offers a choice of ambience. You
can sample their traditional English cooking at a table in their chic main area,
prop up the bar with friends or enjoy a romantic dinner in a room to one side
of the bar. The chef, Calum Franklin, uses the finest British ingredients and
ensures that everything is in season. For example, you can feast on stewed
Suffolk lamb, a simply divine chicken and girolle pie, or smoked haddock
and poached egg accompanied by a mustard sauce. You absolutely have to
taste their Monkshill Farm Scotch Egg, winner of the Scotch Egg Challenge in
2015. You can enjoy lunch or dinner all year round on their delightful terrace,
designed by the famous landscape designer Luciano Giubbilei.

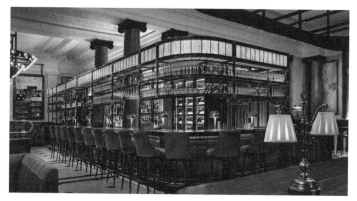

# HOPPERS

49 FRITH ST, SOHO, W1D 4SG

⊖ Leicester Square

**MONDAY–THURSDAY:** midday–2.30 pm/5.30 pm–10.30 pm
**FRIDAY–SATURDAY:** midday–10.30 pm

🦐🦐 to 🦐🦐🦐 depending on the product

`HTTPS://WWW.HOPPERSLONDON.COM`                    🄵 🐦 📷

If you like Indian and Sri Lankan cuisine, this is the place for you! Located in the well-known and lively Frith Street, this is a traditional but far from conventional restaurant. Its décor combines traditional masks with vintage posters and there are some real delicacies on offer. The menu is simple but highly effective, and the service is in tune with the establishment's image: relaxed and welcoming.

The menu offers a number of starters and sides which are richly spiced. For the main course you have a choice of Hopper (a cake soft on the inside and crunchy on the outside in the form of a bowl and made using rice flour) or Dosa (buttered cake made with extra-crunchy ghee), accompanied by a curry to suit your taste: lamb, beef, chicken, fish or vegetarian. The only slight (or major?) drawback is that they don't take bookings. Try to come on a weekday lunchtime. At the weekend, whether lunch- or dinnertime, you are strongly advised to come 20 minutes before opening, because a queue builds up outside the restaurant very quickly. But trust me, it's well worth the hassle!

# THE GREENHOUSE

27A HAY'S MEWS, W1J 5NY
☎ (0)20 7499 3331 ⊖ Green Park

**MONDAY–FRIDAY:** midday–2.30 pm / 6 pm–10.30 pm
**SATURDAY:** 6.30 pm–10.30 pm
🍴🍴🍴🍴

HTTP://WWW.GREENHOUSERESTAURANT.CO.UK                    f y

The Greenhouse is a veritable oasis of calm, right in the heart of residential Mayfair. Your journey begins on your arrival, with a short path bordered by greenery that leads to the restaurant's front door. The restaurant itself is tastefully and elegantly decorated. The welcome and the service are simultaneously warm and discreet. The food by chef Arnaud Bignon is a distillation of fresh and original flavours prepared in an elegant and contemporary way. The harmony of tastes and the balance of his dishes make the whole effect quite simply perfect.

A special mention must be made for the Orkney scallops with green zebra tomatoes and verbena, and also the turbot with matcha tea, lemon and cauliflower.

Dinner at the Greenhouse is a truly timeless experience.

# STORY

199 TOOLEY ST, SE1 2JX

☎ (0)20 7183 2117  ⊖ Bermondsey then bus 381 to bus stop T Boss Street

**MONDAY:** 6.30 pm–10 pm • **TUESDAY–SATURDAY:** midday–5 pm/6.30 pm–10 pm
**SUNDAY:** midday–3 pm/6.30 pm–10 pm
🍱🍱🍱 to 🍱🍱🍱🍱 depending on the product or wine

HTTP://WWW.RESTAURANTSTORY.CO.UK

The décor is pared-down Nordic chic. Geometric and made of stripped-back materials such as wood and brick, it's a light and airy space thanks to an all-round picture window. The food is interesting, technically accomplished in an understated sort of way. The cooking shows the influence of the various kitchens where chef Thomas Keller has worked (such as that of René Redzepi) with a touch of originality all his own. A special mention must be made for the pigeon with summer truffles and pine nuts.

# THE CLOVE CLUB

SHOREDITCH TOWN HALL, 380 OLD ST, EC1V 9LT

☎ (0)20 7729 6496  ⊖ Old Street then bus 55 to bus stop X Shoreditch Town Hall

**MONDAY:** 6.30 pm–11.30 pm • **TUESDAY–SATURDAY:** midday–2.30 pm/6 pm–11.30 pm
Snack menu at the bar : 🍱🍱 • Special menu : 🍱🍱🍱
Food and wine combined : 🍱🍱🍱🍱

HTTP://THECLOVECLUB.COM

Situated in the former Shoreditch town hall, The Clove Club is considered by many to be a rare temple of gastronomy. The décor is disarmingly simple. But this restaurant has been praised by many critics around the world and rated 26th of the top 50 restaurants in the world by San Pellegrino, purely due to the quality of its food! Around a simple menu (meat or vegetarian) chef Isaac McHale has created a cuisine with some quite remarkable seasonings. The restaurant also has a room where you can simply eat snacks (the menu there is quite crazy!)

# HONEY & CO.

25A WARREN ST, W1T 5LZ
☎ (0)20 7388 6175 ⊖ Warren Street

**MONDAY–FRIDAY:** 8 am–10.30 pm · **SATURDAY:** 9.30 am–10.30 pm
🍴🍴

Consult the website for the other location

`HTTP://HONEYANDCO.CO.UK`

We are huge fans of this restaurant. When you take that first bite of whatever it is you're eating, something truly extraordinary happens: you are transported into a world of exceptional flavours and spices! Sarit Packer and Itamar Srulovich, two Israelis who have lived in England for a number of years now, have created a cuisine in their own image: warm and Mediterranean. They like to say it is the cuisine of their mothers, a generous cuisine, full of love. It is beyond heavenly, made up of colourful dishes with exotic tastes. Throughout the week the restaurant offers superb breakfasts with Middle Eastern flavours such as sabich (grilled aubergines, eggs, sesame sauce, zaatar and pitta bread) and roasted goat's cheese with sage and crusty bread. On Saturdays they serve a sort of brunch, the 'big breakfast', which will really cover your whole tabletop. You are strongly recommended to book, as the restaurant is not very big.

# CÉLESTE

LANESBOROUGH HOTEL - HYDE PARK CORNER, SW1X 7TA
☎ (0)20 7259 5599 ⊖ Hyde Park Corner

**MONDAY–SUNDAY:** midday–2.30 pm/7 pm–10.30 pm
🍲🍲🍲🍲

HTTP://WWW.LANESBOROUGH.COM/ENG/RESTAURANT-BARS/CELESTE/

With a décor reminiscent of an English stately home, complete with sublime mouldings and tinkling chandeliers, you can sample the cuisine of the triple-Michelin-starred Éric Fréchon and his executive chef Florian Favario. The food draws inspiration from traditional French know-how while preserving the authenticity of the finest British produce, for example: roast suckling pig with crushed potatoes, or stuffed lamb with spring vegetables and red pepper coulis. The real originality of this restaurant comes from their lunchtime and dinnertime vegetarian gastronomic menu. This will surprise you with some incredible dishes, such as courgette flowers with fresh goat's cheese and smoked tomatoes, or artichoke barigoule. This technically accomplished and refined menu will definitely give you an opportunity to take the measure of Éric Fréchon's culinary virtuosity.

# MAZI

12-14 HILLGATE ST, W8 7SR
☎ (0)20 7229 3794   ⊖ Notting Hill Gate

**MONDAY:** 6.30 pm–10.30 pm  •  **TUESDAY–SATURDAY:** midday–3 pm/6.30 pm–10.30 pm  **SUNDAY:** midday–3 pm/6.30 pm–10 pm

🍲🍲 to 🍲🍲🍲

HTTP://WWW.MAZI.CO.UK                                              f ⊙

Mazi, which is Greek for 'together', is an ode to Greek cuisine. The food here is synonymous with that tradition, with basic emblematic dishes such as tzatziki and meatballs, to which they add a twist of modernity in order to show the world how Greek cuisine can be innovative, tasty and refined. That is the case with their feta tempura with lemon marmalade and caper meringue, or their brisket of lamb with aubergines coated in miso, chick peas and tahini. The restaurant pays particular attention to sourcing its produce, with most of it imported directly from Greece, where they buy stock from small local producers. In summer you can eat outside in their charming little garden.

# LYLE'S

TEA BUILDING, 56 SHOREDITCH HIGH ST, E1 6JJ

☎ (0)20 3011 5911  ⊖ Liverpool Street Station then bus 26 or 48 from bus stop F
Liverpool Street Station to F Shoreditch High Street/Bethnal Green Road

**MONDAY–FRIDAY:** 8 am–11 pm • **SATURDAY:** midday–midnight
🍴🍴 to 🍴🍴🍴 depending on the product

HTTP://LYLESLONDON.COM

The style of this restaurant is quite simple and pared-down, and the food
is similarly characterised by its simplicity and finesse. For lunch you have a
choice of various small dishes each as colourful and flavoursome as the next,
such as, for example, asparagus with bacon and nuts, sweetbreads with radishes and molasses, razor clams and seaweed cake or caramel and meringue
ice cream with coffee. In the evenings they offer a four-course menu.

# POLPO

41 BEAK ST, W1F 9SB
☎ (0)20 7734 4479  ⊖ Piccadilly Circus or Oxford Circus

MONDAY–FRIDAY: 11.30 am-11 pm  •  SATURDAY: 10 am–11 pm
SUNDAY: 10 am–10 pm
🍲🍲 to 🍲🍲🍲 depending on the product

Consult the website for other locations

HTTP://WWW.POLPO.CO.UK

Polpo is a bàcaro, which is a Venetian word describing an unpretentious restaurant that provides simple cooking and good Italian wines. Polpo offers charming tapas such as arancini, lamb meatballs with pistachio, pork belly with apricot and sage, and mini pizzas with ricotta and salami flavoured with fennel, all washed down with an Italian wine or a Spritz, that famous venetian cocktail made of prosecco, soda water and either Campari® or Aperol®. At weekends they serve different dishes for brunch, such as their scrambled egg and smoked salmon tart.

# MIRROR ROOM

ROSEWOOD HOTEL, 252 HIGH HOLBORN, WC1V 7EN
☎ (0)20 3747 8620 ⊖ Holborn

**MONDAY–SUNDAY:** 7 am–11 am (breakfast) • **MONDAY–SUNDAY:** 11 am–10 pm
(lunch–dinner) • **MONDAY–SUNDAY:** midday–7 pm (tea)

HTTP://WWW.ROSEWOODHOTELS.COM/EN/LONDON/DINING/MIRROR-ROOM

Located in the splendid Rosewood Hotel, the Mirror Room is a real gem. As its name suggests, its walls are covered with mirrors, which makes this superb dining room feel even bigger, without detracting from the cosy ambience provided by the soft lighting and the comfortable banquettes. The restaurant offers an elegant but relaxed dining experience, and the service is welcoming and accessible, exactly in the image of its chef, Amandine Chaignot. Having worked in some of the grandest Parisian establishments, such as Le Meurice and Le Crillon, Amandine Chaignot offers a cuisine of notable nuance and technical subtlety with a respect for the product at its heart. Eating here is a full-on sensory and emotional experience. A herb might bring to mind a walk in the forest, a fruit might be prepared in such a way that it awakens childhood memories, or a sauce might be reminiscent of a journey you have made in the past. Amandine Chaignot is one of those rare chefs who is able to offer the intangible: pure emotion.

# OLDROYD

344 UPPER ST, N1 0PD
☎ (0)20 8617 9010  ⊖ Angel

MONDAY–THURSDAY: midday–11 pm  •  FRIDAY–SATURDAY: midday–11.30 pm
SUNDAY: 11 am–9.30 pm
🍴🍴 to 🍴🍴🍴 depending on the product

HTTP://WWW.OLDROYDLONDON.COM

The chef, Tom Oldroyd, is no novice: he was formerly the head chef at the
Polpo restaurants in London. Oldroyd's vision is clear and direct, with dishes
influenced by European cuisine (steak tartare with anchovies and egg-yolk
French toast, or seafood fritto misto with blood orange) created with
British produce. The Sunday brunch is exceptional – very refined and original. It combines the classics of the English breakfast with perfectly executed
bistro food. You are strongly recommended to book, as the restaurant is not
very big.

# OTTOLENGHI

50 ARTILLERY LANE, E1 7LJ

☎ (0)20 7247 1999  ⊖ Aldgate East then bus 67 from bus stop F Aldgate East Station to Brushfield Street

**MONDAY–FRIDAY:** 8 am–10.30 pm  •  **SATURDAY:** 9 am–10.30 pm
**SUNDAY:** 9 am–6 pm
🍱🍱 to 🍱🍱🍱 depending on the product

Consult the website for other locations

HTTP://WWW.OTTOLENGHI.CO.UK

Even though you can eat meat in his restaurants, Yotam Ottolenghi is nonetheless God Almighty when it comes to vegetarian cuisine! As soon as you walk through the door, the salad buffets take you straight to where it's at. Ottolenghi draws on oriental influences and skilfully combines seasoning, spices, oils and vegetables of every sort. Every dish is an explosion of flavours. For example, the shakshuka on the breakfast menu is simply irresistible. It tastes exactly as it does in the markets of Tel Aviv or Jerusalem. Likewise for the salad of aubergines, labneh, pistachios and herbs, or the lamb keftas with crystallised lemon, garlic yogurt and parsley oil. Eating in one of Yotam Ottolenghi's restaurants is like going on a journey.

# SMOKEHOUSE

63-69 CANONBURY RD, ISLINGTON, N1 2DG
☎ (0)20 7354 1144  ⊖ Highbury & Islington

**MONDAY–FRIDAY:** 6 pm-10 pm  •  **SATURDAY:** midday–4 pm/6 pm–10 pm
**SUNDAY:** midday–9 pm
🎲🎲 to 🎲🎲🎲 depending on the product

HTTP://SMOKEHOUSEISLINGTON.CO.UK

Smokehouse resides in a brick house in Islington. Simply decorated using stripped-back materials, its food too is appropriately simple, homely and comforting. The food is cooked, roasted, grilled or smoked. The smoked duck stew with tagliatelle is simply divine, as is their sticky toffee pudding with caramel bourbon. On Sundays you shouldn't miss their excellent Sunday roast.

## Key to symbols

○ interchange stations

Ⓢ Step-free access from street to train

Ⓐ Step-free access from street to platform

≠ National Rail

🚢 Riverboat services

✈ Airport

🚎 Victoria Coach Station

🚠 Emirates Air Line cable car

## Explanation of zones

| 9 | Station in Zone 9 |
| 8 | Station in Zone 8 |
| 7 | Station in Zone 7 |
| 6 | Station in Zone 6 |
| 5 | Station in Zone 5 |
| 4 | Station in both zones |
| 4 | Station in Zone 4 |
| 3 | Station in both zones |
| 3 | Station in Zone 3 |
| 2 | Station in both zones |
| 2 | Station in Zone 2 |
| 1 | Station in both zones |
| 1 | Station in Zone 1 |

© Transport for London   June 2016

# INDEX

**Dandelyan 79**
Mondrian London Hotel - 20 Upper
Ground, SE1 9PD

**DF Mexico 82**
28-29 Tottenham Court Rd, W1T 1BL
15 Hanbury St, E1 6QR

**Dinerama 86**
19 Great Eastern St, EC2A 3EJ
Consult the website for
other locations

**Dirty Bones 71**
20 Kensington Church St, W8 4EP
Top Floor, Kingly Court, Carnaby St, Soho,
W1B 5PW

**Dominique Ansel 45**
17-21 Elizabeth St, Belgravia, SW1W 9RP

# E - F

**E Pellicci 62**
332 Bethnal Green Rd, E2 0AG

**F. Cooke 85**
9 Broadway Market, E8 4PH

**Fabrique Bakery 54**
8 Earlham St, WC2H 9RY
212 Portobello Road, W11 1LA
Consult the website for other locations

**Fortnum & Mason 12**
181 Piccadilly, W1A 1ER

**Foxcroft & Ginger 62**
69-79 Mile End Rd, E1 4TT

**Frenchie 100**
16 Henrietta Street, WC2E 8QH

# G

**Gail's Bakery 56**
SOHO 128 Wardour St., W1F 8ZL
Consult the website for the other locations

**Gill Wing Cook Shop 15**
190 Upper St, N1 1RQ
Consult the website for other location

**Global kitchen à Camden
Market 34**
54-56 Camden Lock Place, NW1 8AF

**Granger & Co. 104**
Stanley Building, 7 Pancras Square,
N1C 4AG
Consult the website for other locations

# H

**Harrods 16**
87-135 Brompton Rd, SW1X 7XL

**Holborn Dining Room 106**
Hotel Rosewood - 252 High Holborn,
WC1V 7EN

**Honey & Co 111**
25a Warren St, W1T 5LZ

**Hook 88**
63-65 Parkway, Camden, NW1 7PP

**Hoppers 107**
49 Frith St, Soho, W1D 4SG

# L

**La Fromagerie 18**
2-6 Moxon St, W1U 4EW
Consult the website for other locations

**Lardo 85**
197-201 Richmond Rd, E8 3NJ

**Lyle's 114**
Tea Building, 56 Shoreditch High St, E1 6JJ

# M

**Maitre Choux 58**
15 Harrington Rd, Kensington, SW7 3ES

**Maltby Street Market 36**
Lassco Ropewalk, 41 Maltby St, SE1 3PA

**Marylebone Farmers' Market 33**
Cramer Street Car Park, Marylebone,
W1U 4EW
Consult the website for other locations

**Mazi 113**
12-14 Hillgate St, W8 7SR

**Mercato Metropolitano 40**
42 Newington Causeway, SE1 6DR

**Mirror Room 116**
Rosewood Hotel - 252 High Holborn,
WC1V 7EN

**My Cup of Tea 11**
5 Denman Pl., W1D 7AH

# N

**Nanban 92**
426 Coldharbour Lane, SW9 8LF

**Neal's Yard Dairy 22**
Covent garden shop, 17 Shorts Gardens,
WC2H 9AT
Borough market shop, 6 Park St, SE1 9AB
Consult the website for other locations

# O

**Oldroyd 118**
344 Upper St, N1 0PD

**Ottolenghi 119**
50 Artillery Lane, E1 7LJ
Consult the website for other locations

# P

**Pavilion Bakery 55**
18 Broadway Market, E8 4QJ

**Paxton & Whitfield 14**
93 Jermyn St, SW1Y 6JE
Consult the website for
other location

**Peggy Porschen Cakes 46**
116 Ebury St, SW1W 9QQ

**Pizza East 93**
56 Shoreditch High St, E1 6JJ
Consult the website for other locations

**Polpo 115**
41 Beak St, W1F 9SB
Consult the website for other locations

**Pop Brixton 39**
49 Brixton Station Rd, SW9 8PQ

**Poppie's Fish & Chips 90**
6-8 Hanbury St, E1 6QR
30 Hawley Crescent, NW1 8NP
55 Old Compton St, W1D 6HW

# R - S

**Rococo Chocolates 21**
5 Motcomb St, SW1X 8JU
3 Moxon St, W1U 4EW
Consult the website for other locations

**St. John Bread and Wine 66**
94-96 Commercial St, E1 6LZ
Consult the website for other locations

**Salon 103**
18 Market Row, Brixton, SW9 8LD

**Selfridges Foodhall 20**
400 Oxford St, W1A 1AB

**Sketch 48**
9 Conduit St, W1S 2XG

**Smokehouse 120**
63-69 Canonbury Rd, Islington, N1 2DG

**Spa Terminus 38**
Dockley Road Industrial Estate, Dockley Rd,
SE16 3SF

**Story 110**
199 Tooley St, SE1 2JX

# T

**The Breakfast Club 66**
31 Camden Passage, N1 8EA
Consult the website for other locations

**The Clove Club 110**
Shoreditch Town Hall, 380 Old St, EC1V 9LT

**The Colony Grill Room 63**
The Beaumont Hotel – 8 Balderton St,
Brown Hart Gardens, Mayfair, W1K 6TF

**The Ginstitute 76**
Portobello Star - 171 Portobello Rd,
W11 2DY

**The Greenhouse 108**
27a Hay's Mews, W1J 5NY

**The Lyric 74**
37 Great Windmill St, W1D 7LU

**The Mayfair Chippy 89**
14 N Audley St, W1K 6WE

**The Shepherdess Café 67**
221 City Rd, EC1V 1JN

**The Spice Shop 24**
1 Blenheim Crescent, W11 2EE

**The Spread Eagle 75**
141 Albert St, NW1 7NB

**The Sun tavern 75**
66 Long Acre, WC2E 9JD

**Three Eight Four 78**
384 Coldharbour Lane, SW9 8LF

**Turner & George 25**
399 St John St, Clerkenwell, EC1V 4LB

# U - W

**Udderlicious 57**
187 Upper St, N1 1RQ

**Whole Foods Market 23**
63-97 Kensington High St, The Barkers
Building, W8 5SE
Consult the website for other locations

# ACKNOWLEDGEMENTS

To my daughter Juliette, because being part of her life is without doubt the best thing in my life. My desire to see the world is driven by the need to find the best way to help you discover it.

To Marie Baumann, for her kindness and the touch of madness that led her to believe in this project but which above all has sustained it with so much passion. Never stop telling me to 'stop', because that means you must be by my side.

To Sophie Greloux and Isabelle Raimond for their amazing work, their kindness, their support, their gentle words. Girls, you are magic!

To James Elliott and Lisa Magano, thanks for always being nearby and for making these projects what they are. I particularly value your capacity to smile in the face of adversity and your enthusiasm.

To Mathieu Persan, my brother, your cover designs really blow me away! I thank you from the bottom of my heart for sharing your immense talent with me.

To Olivier Goujon for his support, help and understanding.

To Émilie Fléchaire for her valued friendship and illuminating ideas.

To Élodie Piège, Jacques Chaniol, Walter Delazoppa and Alexandra Hurtes. All your words of encouragement during these months of travel to the far side of the world prove to me definitively that our friendship has no limits.

To my parents, my family and my friends, whom I have neglected these last few months, whom I have stood up, whose birthdays I have forgotten, with whom I have shared a tear, or to whom I have spoken harshly when having a bad day.

This guide book would not have been possible without the help of Amandine Chaignot. My friend, thank you for putting your house and your herbal teas at my disposal with no strings attached. Thank you from the bottom of my heart for everything and more besides.

Graphic design: Lisa Magano
Editorial coordinator: Sophie Greloux